SELECTIONS FROM O BROTHER, WHERE ART THOU?

Artwork and photos courtesy of Touchstone Pictures

Music transcriptions by Pete Billmann

ISBN 0-634-03155-4

HAL•LEONARD® CORPORATION

7777 W. BLUEMOUND RD. P.O. BOX 13819 MILWAUKEE, WI 53213

Visit Hal Leonard Online at
www.halleonard.com

CONTENTS

The Big Rock Candy Mountain

Words, Music and Arrangement by Harry McClintock

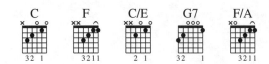

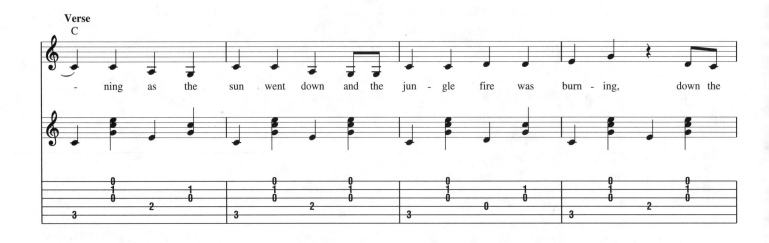

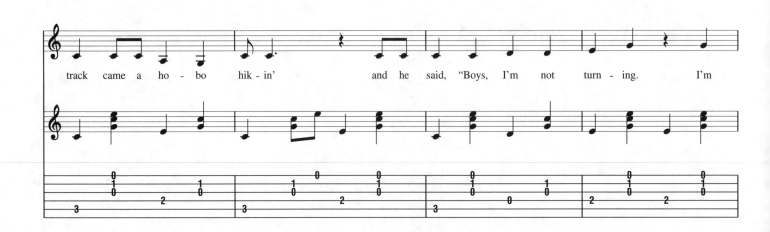

head-ed for a land that's far a-way, ___ be-sides the crys-tal foun-tains. So

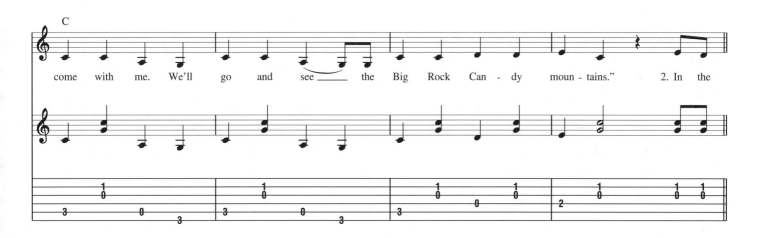

come with me. We'll go and see ___ the Big Rock Can-dy moun-tains." 2. In the

Verse

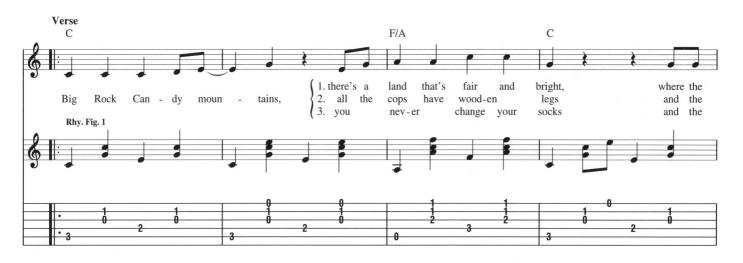

Big Rock Can-dy moun - tains,

1. there's a land that's fair and bright, where the
2. all the cops have wood-en legs and the
3. you nev-er change your socks and the

Rhy. Fig. 1

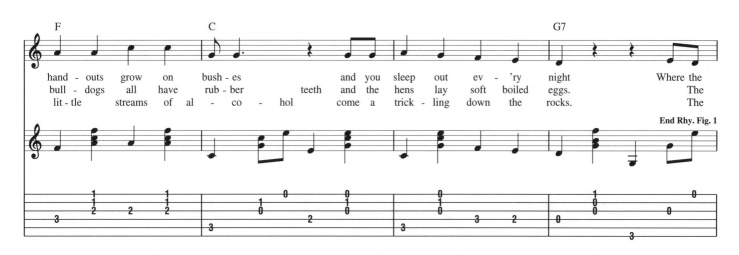

hand - outs grow on bush - es and you sleep out ev - 'ry night Where the
bull - dogs all have rub - ber teeth and the hens lay soft boiled eggs. The
lit - tle streams of al - co - hol come a trick - ling down the rocks. The

End Rhy. Fig. 1

9

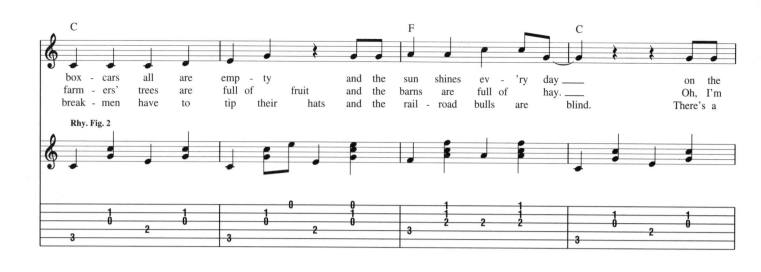

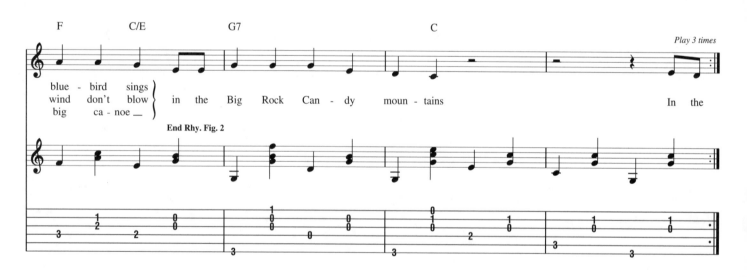

no short han-dled shov-els, no ax-es, saws or picks. I'm a

go-in' to stay ___ where you sleep all day, where they hung the jerk that in-

Gtr. 1

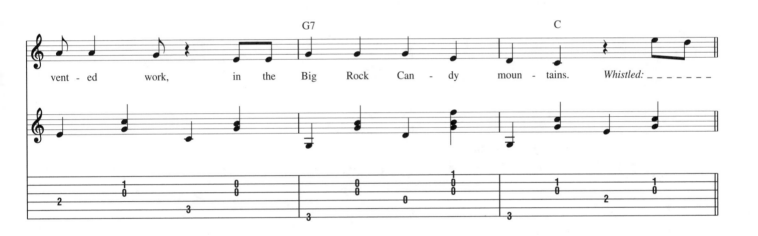

vent-ed work, in the Big Rock Can-dy moun-tains. *Whistled:* _ _ _ _ _ _ _

Outro

Gtr. 1: w/ Rhy. Fig. 2

_ I'll

see you all this com-in' fall ___ in the Big Rock Can-dy moun-tains.

Gtr. 1

You Are My Sunshine

Words and Music by Jimmie Davis and Charles Mitchell

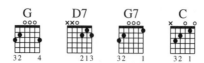

Gtr. 1: Open G tuning, down 1/2 step:
(low to high) Gb–Bb–Db–Gb–Bb–Db
Gtrs. 2 & 3: Tune down 1/2 step:
(low to high) Eb–Ab–Db–Gb–Bb–Eb

take my   sun - shine   a -   way.

Dobro Solo

Verse

love ____ you _____ and make you ___ hap - py   if you ___ will on - - ly
dreams, _ dear, _____ you seem to ___ leave me.   When I ____ a - wake my

say _____ the _____ same.   But if ___ you leave me _____ and love an -
poor _____ heart ____ pains.   So won't you come back _____ and make me

- oth - er,   you'll re - gret _____ it all _____ some day.
hap - py.   I'll for - give, dear, I'll take all the blame.

Chorus
Gtr. 2: w/ Rhy. Fig. 1

You are ___ my sun - shine,   my ___ on - ly ___ sun - shine.   You make _ me hap -

- py _____ when skies are gray. _____   You'll nev - er know, ___ dear, _____

___ how _ much I love ___ you.   Please don't take my _____ sun - shine a - way.

Mandolin Solo
Gtr. 2: w/ Rhy. Fig. 1

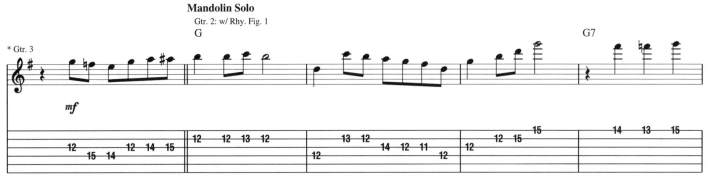

* Mandolin arr. for gtr.

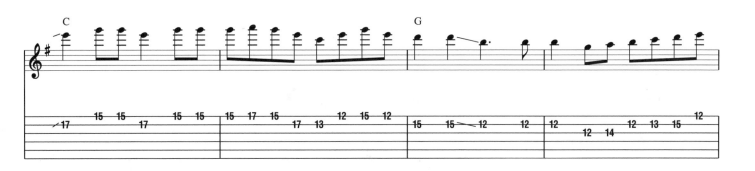

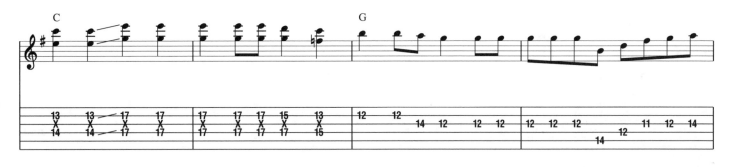

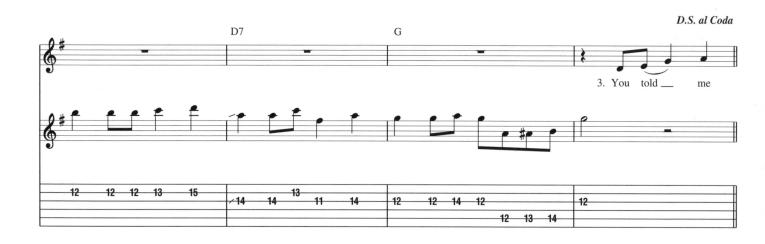

3. You told ___ me

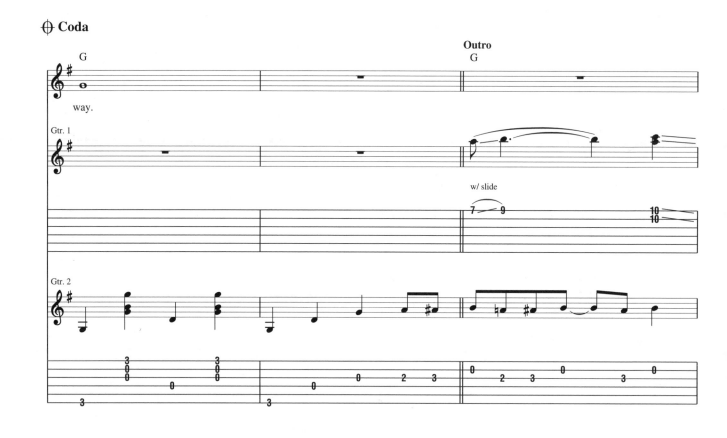

Coda

Outro

way.

Gtr. 1

w/ slide

Gtr. 2

w/o slide

I Am a Man of Constant Sorrow

Words and Music by Carter Stanley

Gtr. 1: Drop D tuning, Capo III:
(low to high) D–A–D–G–B–E

Intro

Moderately ♩ = 88

* Symbols in parentheses represent chord names respective to capoed guitar
Symbols above reflect actual sounting chord. Capoed fret is "0" in tab.

Verse

Rhy. Fig. 1

1. I _____ am a man _____ of con - stant

17

Hard Time Killing Floor Blues

Words and Music by Nehemiah "Skip" James

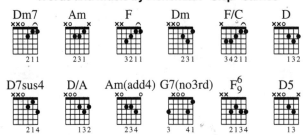

Gtr. 1: Open Dm tuning:
(low to high) D–A–D–F–A–D

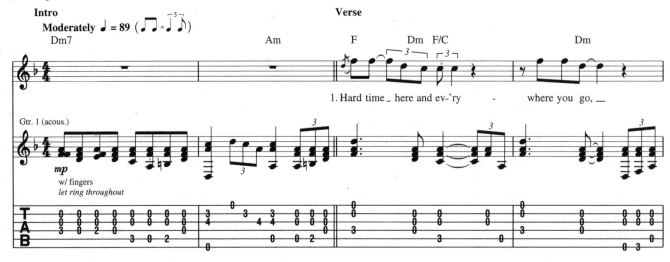

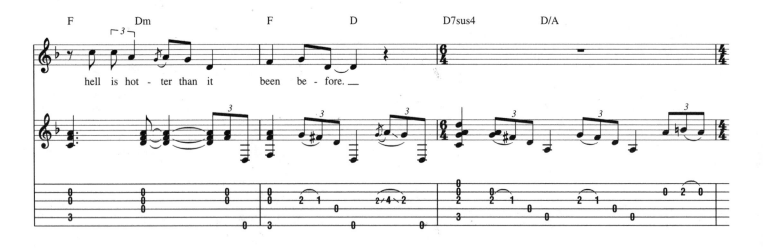

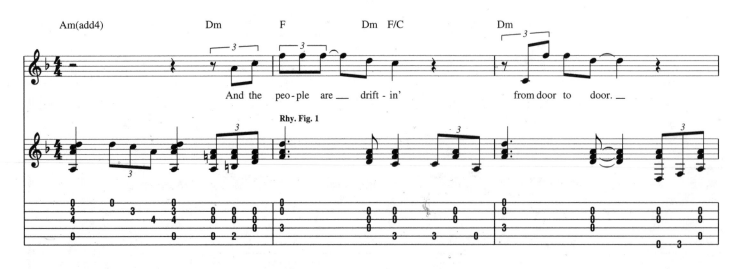

Keep on the Sunny Side

Words and Music by A.P. Carter

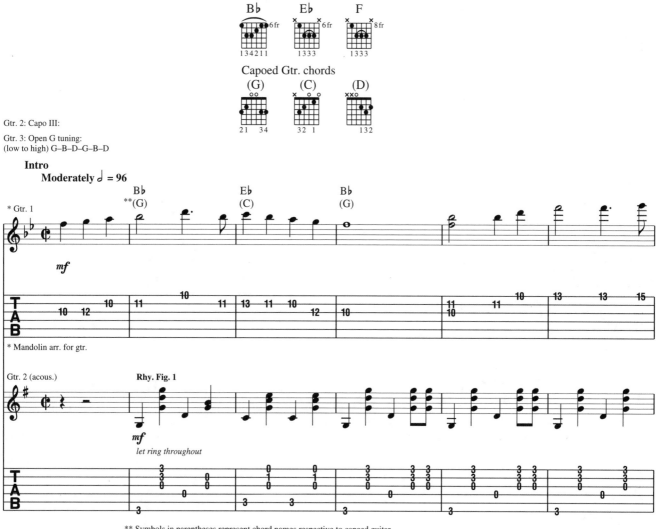

Gtr. 2: Capo III:

Gtr. 3: Open G tuning:
(low to high) G–B–D–G–B–D

Intro
Moderately ♩ = 96

* Gtr. 1

mf

* Mandolin arr. for gtr.

Gtr. 2 (acous.)

Rhy. Fig. 1

mf

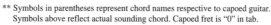
let ring throughout

** Symbols in parentheses represent chord names respective to capoed guitar.
Symbols above reflect actual sounding chord. Capoed fret is "0" in tab.

D.S. al Coda 2

Coda 2

Chorus

Keep on the sun-ny side, al - ways on the sun-ny ___ side. Keep on the sun-ny side of life. It will help ___ us ev - 'ry day, ___ it will bright-en all ___ the way if we'll keep on the sun-ny side of life. If we'll keep on the sun - ny side of life.

I Am a Man of Constant Sorrow

Words and Music by Carter Stanley

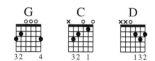

I'll Fly Away

Words and Music by Albert E. Brumley

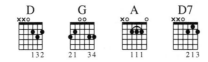

* Mandolin arr. for gtr.

** T = Thumb on 6th string

1. Some ___ bright _____ morn - in' ___ when this life is o'er, _____
2. When ___ the _____ sha - dows ___ of this life have gone, _____
3. Oh, _____ how _____ glad ___ and ___ hap - py when _ we ___ meet, _____

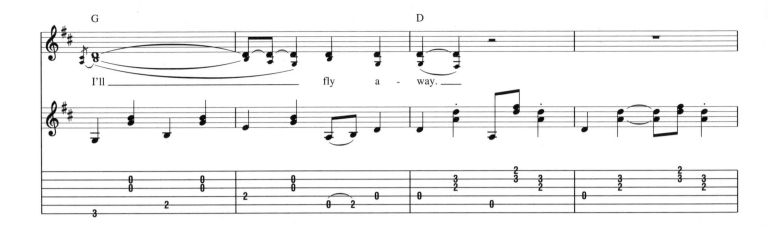

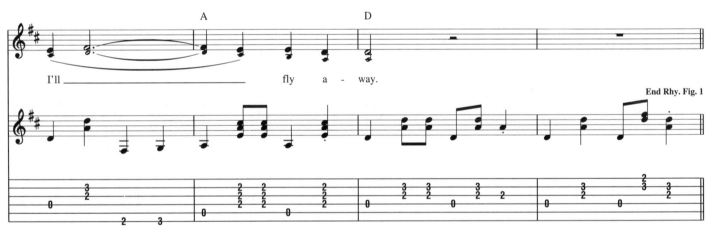

fly a - way in the mornin'. When I die, hal - le - lu -

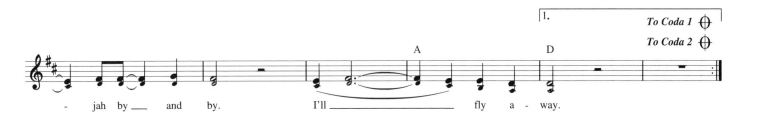

1.
To Coda 1
To Coda 2

- jah by and by. I'll fly a - way.

Mandolin Solo
Gtr. 2: w/ Rhy. Fig. 1

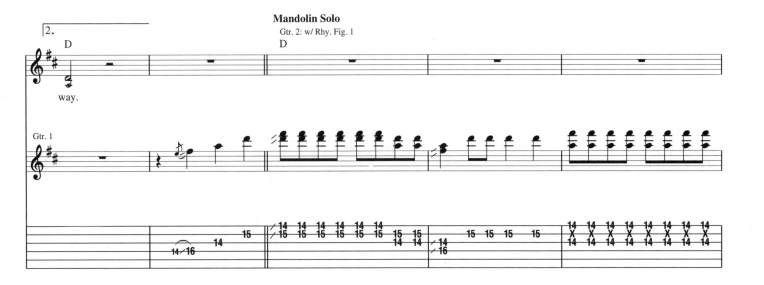

2.
way.

Gtr. 1

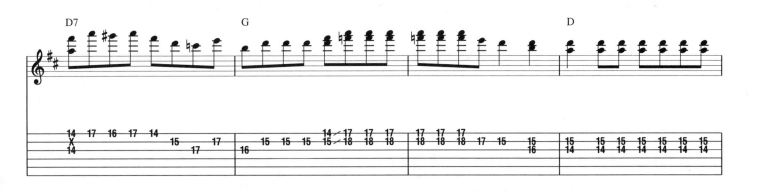

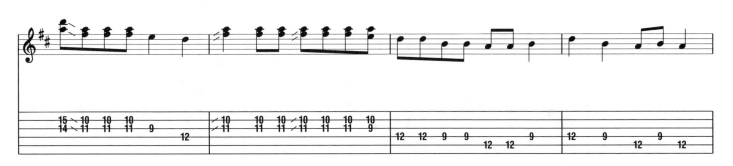

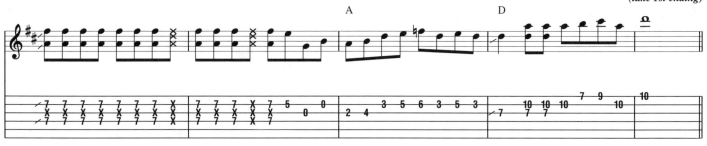

⊕ Coda 1

Mandolin Solo

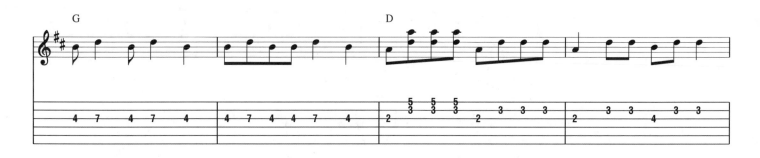

D.S.S. al Coda 2
(take 1st ending)

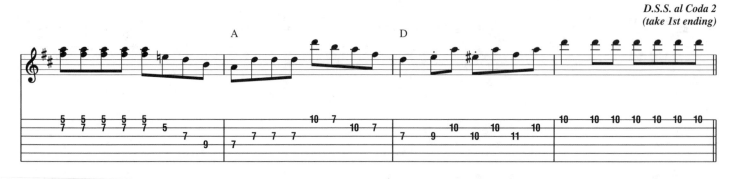

⊕ Coda 2

Verse

4. Just   a   few   more   wear-y   days ___   and   then _____   I'll _____

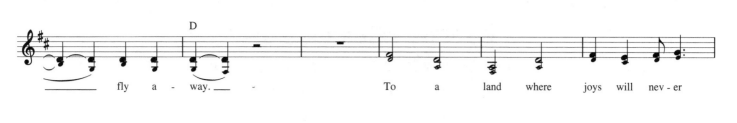

fly a - way. ___ - To a land where joys will nev - er

Chorus
Gtr. 2: w/ Rhy. Fig. 1

end, _____ I'll _____ fly a - way. I'll _____
(I'll fly a -

___ fly a - way, oh glo - ry, I'll _____ fly a -
way.)

way ___ in the morn - in'. When I die, hal - le - lu - jah by ___ and

by. I'll _____ fly a - way.

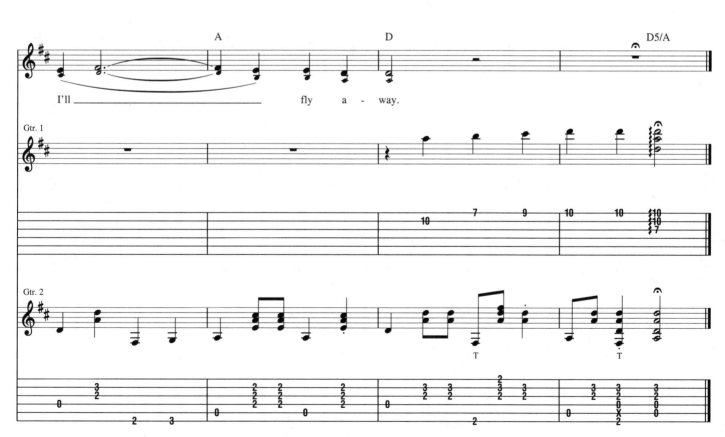

I'll _____ fly a - way.

Gtr. 1

Gtr. 2

In the Highways
(I'll Be Somewhere Working for My Lord)

Words and Music by Maybelle Carter

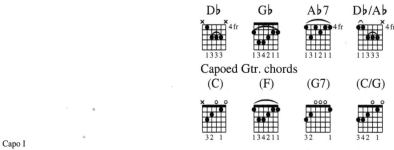

Capoed Gtr. chords
(C)   (F)   (G7)   (C/G)

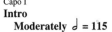

Intro
Moderately ♩ = 115

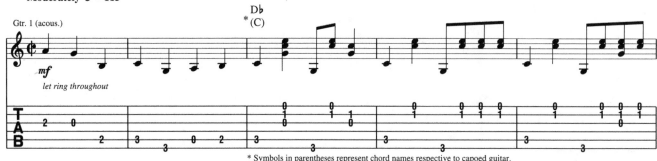

** Symbols in parentheses represent chord names respective to capoed guitar.
Symbols above reflect actual sounding chord. Capoed fret is "0" in tab.*

%$ Verse

1. In the high - ways in the hedg - es, in the high - ways in the hedg -

calls ___ me, I will an -

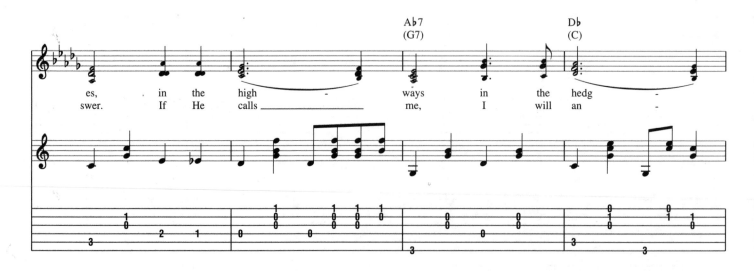

swer. If He calls ___ me, I will an -

2nd time, Gtr. 1: w/ Fill 1
3rd time, Gtr. 1: w/ Fill 2

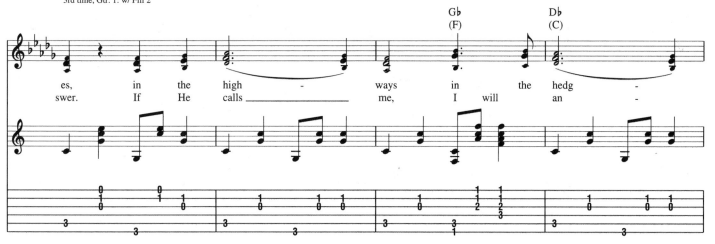

es,   in the high   ways   in   the   hedg -
swer.   If He calls _____ me,   I   will   an -

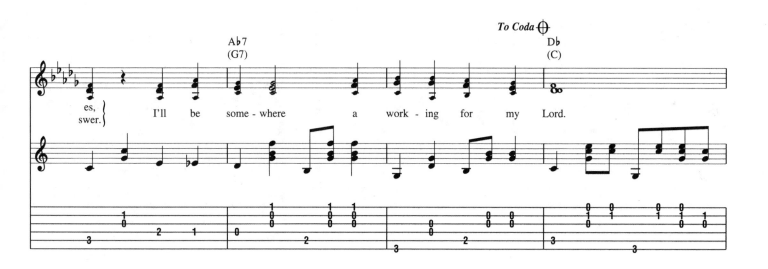

es,
swer.   I'll   be   some - where   a   work - ing   for   my   Lord.

Chorus

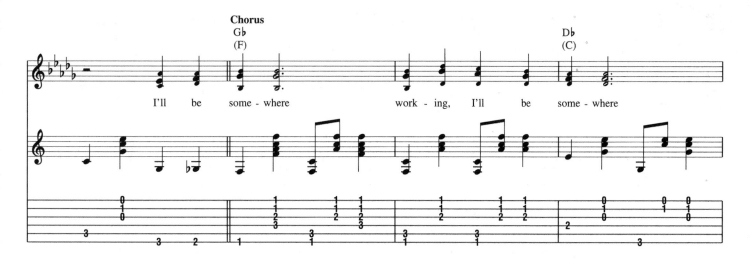

I'll   be   some - where   work - ing,   I'll   be   some - where

Fill 1
Gtr. 1

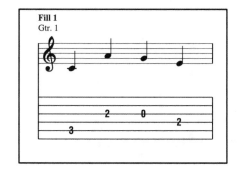

Fill 2
Gtr. 1

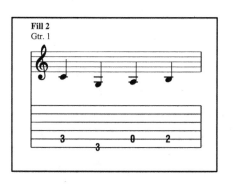

37

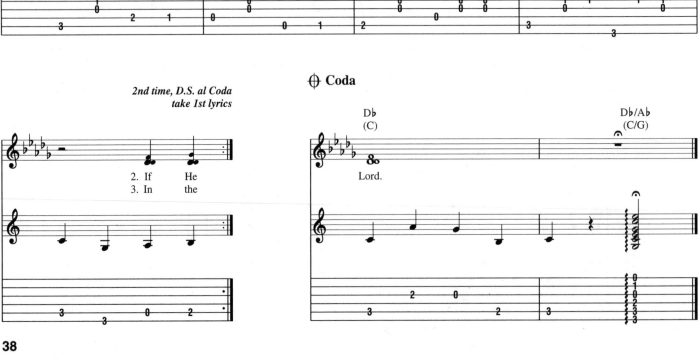

I Am Weary (Let Me Rest)

Words and Music by Pete (Roberts) Kuykendall

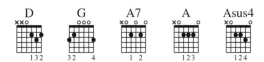

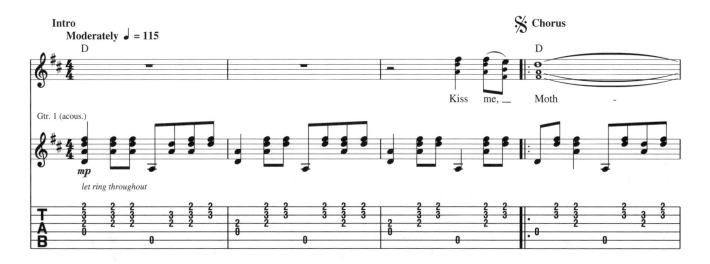

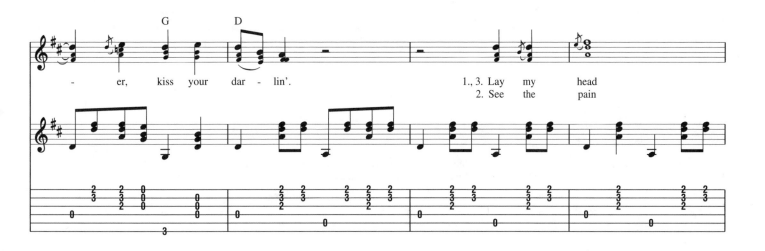

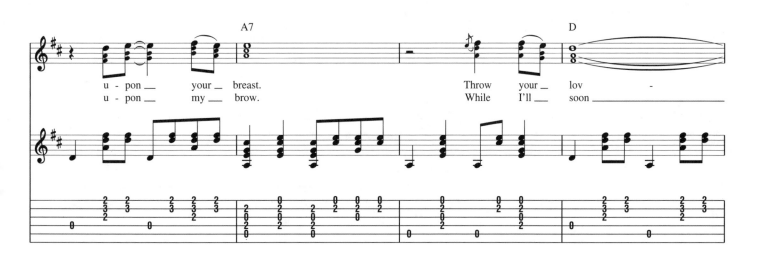

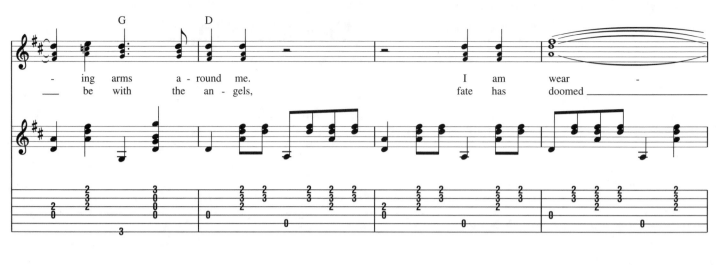

-ing arms a - round me.
___ be with the an - gels,

I am wear -
fate has doomed ___

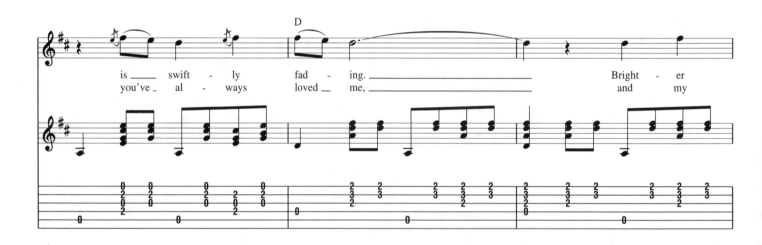

To Coda ⊕

Verse

-y, let me rest.
___ my fu - ture now.

1. Seems the light
2. Through the years

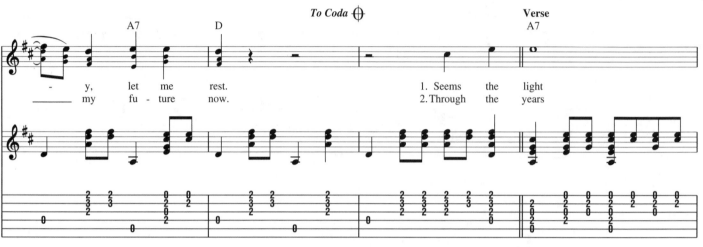

is ___ swift - ly fad - ing. ___
you've ___ al - ways loved ___ me, ___

Bright - er
and my

scenes they do ___ now show.
life you've tried ___ to save.

40

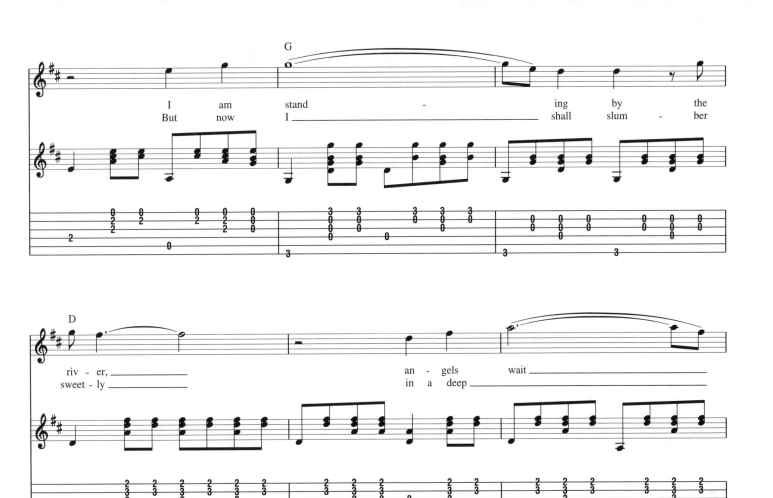

I am stand - - - ing by the
But now I shall slum - ber

riv - er, an - gels wait
sweet - ly in a deep

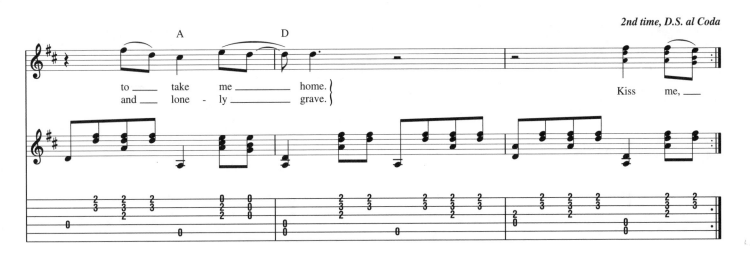

2nd time, D.S. al Coda

to take me home. }
and lone - ly grave. }

Kiss me,

Coda

A   D
rit.

I am wear - y, let me rest.

rit.

41

In the Jailhouse Now

Words and Music by Jimmie Rodgers

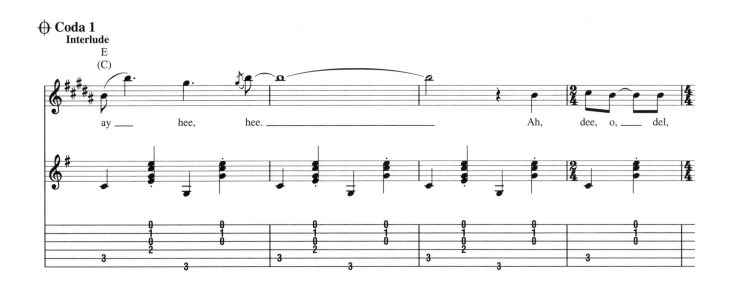

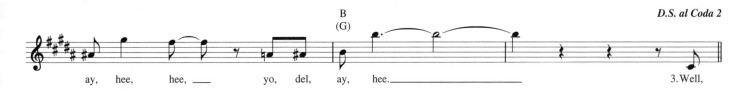

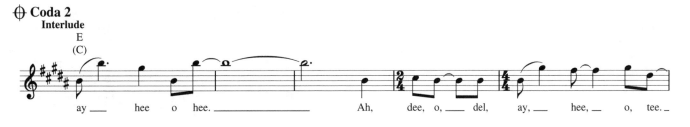

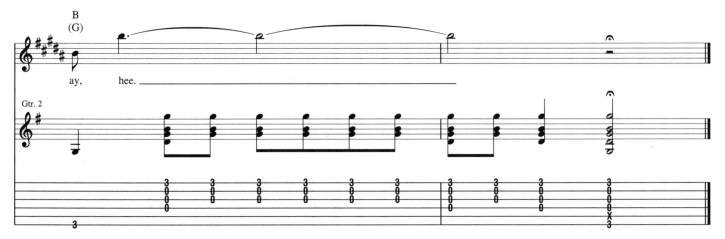

Guitar Notation Legend

Guitar Music can be notated three different ways: on a *musical staff*, in *tablature*, and in *rhythm slashes*.

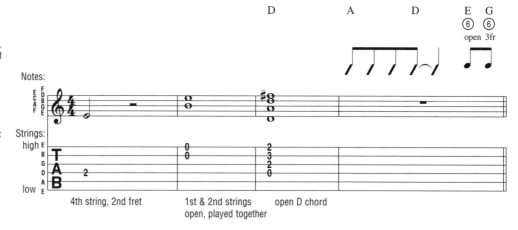

RHYTHM SLASHES are written above the staff. Strum chords in the rhythm indicated. Use the chord diagrams found at the top of the first page of the transcription for the appropriate chord voicings. Round noteheads indicate single notes.

THE MUSICAL STAFF shows pitches and rhythms and is divided by bar lines into measures. Pitches are named after the first seven letters of the alphabet.

TABLATURE graphically represents the guitar fingerboard. Each horizontal line represents a a string, and each number represents a fret.

4th string, 2nd fret   1st & 2nd strings open, played together   open D chord

Definitions for Special Guitar Notation

HALF-STEP BEND: Strike the note and bend up 1/2 step.

WHOLE-STEP BEND: Strike the note and bend up one step.

GRACE NOTE BEND: Strike the note and immediately bend up as indicated.

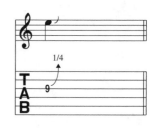

SLIGHT (MICROTONE) BEND: Strike the note and bend up 1/4 step.

BEND AND RELEASE: Strike the note and bend up as indicated, then release back to the original note. Only the first note is struck.

PRE-BEND: Bend the note as indicated, then strike it.

PRE-BEND AND RELEASE: Bend the note as indicated. Strike it and release the bend back to the original note.

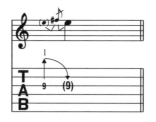

UNISON BEND: Strike the two notes simultaneously and bend the lower note up to the pitch of the higher.

VIBRATO: The string is vibrated by rapidly bending and releasing the note with the fretting hand.

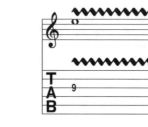

WIDE VIBRATO: The pitch is varied to a greater degree by vibrating with the fretting hand.

HAMMER-ON: Strike the first (lower) note with one finger, then sound the higher note (on the same string) with another finger by fretting it without picking.

PULL-OFF: Place both fingers on the notes to be sounded. Strike the first note and without picking, pull the finger off to sound the second (lower) note.

LEGATO SLIDE: Strike the first note and then slide the same fret-hand finger up or down to the second note. The second note is not struck.

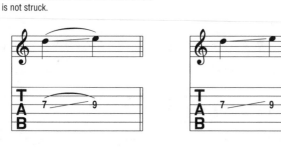

SHIFT SLIDE: Same as legato slide, except the second note is struck.

TRILL: Very rapidly alternate between the notes indicated by continuously hammering on and pulling off.

TAPPING: Hammer ("tap") the fret indicated with the pick-hand index or middle finger and pull off to the note fretted by the fret hand.

NATURAL HARMONIC: Strike the note while the fret-hand lightly touches the string directly over the fret indicated.

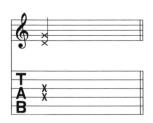

PINCH HARMONIC: The note is fretted normally and a harmonic is produced by adding the edge of the thumb or the tip of the index finger of the pick hand to the normal pick attack.

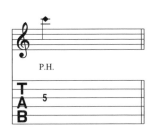

HARP HARMONIC: The note is fretted normally and a harmonic is produced by gently resting the pick hand's index finger directly above the indicated fret (in parentheses) while the pick hand's thumb or pick assists by plucking the appropriate string.

PICK SCRAPE: The edge of the pick is rubbed down (or up) the string, producing a scratchy sound.

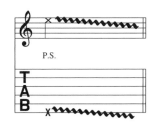

MUFFLED STRINGS: A percussive sound is produced by laying the fret hand across the string(s) without depressing, and striking them with the pick hand.

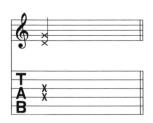

PALM MUTING: The note is partially muted by the pick hand lightly touching the string(s) just before the bridge.

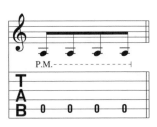

RAKE: Drag the pick across the strings indicated with a single motion.

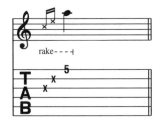

TREMOLO PICKING: The note is picked as rapidly and continuously as possible.

ARPEGGIATE: Play the notes of the chord indicated by quickly rolling them from bottom to top.

VIBRATO BAR DIVE AND RETURN: The pitch of the note or chord is dropped a specified number of steps (in rhythm) then returned to the original pitch.

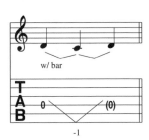

VIBRATO BAR SCOOP: Depress the bar just before striking the note, then quickly release the bar.

VIBRATO BAR DIP: Strike the note and then immediately drop a specified number of steps, then release back to the original pitch.

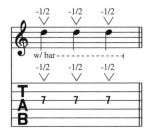

Additional Musical Definitions

 (accent) • Accentuate note (play it louder)

 (accent) • Accentuate note with great intensity

 (staccato) • Play the note short

 • Downstroke

V • Upstroke

D.S. al Coda • Go back to the sign (𝄋), then play until the measure marked "***To Coda***," then skip to the section labelled "**Coda**."

D.C. al Fine • Go back to the beginning of the song and play until the measure marked "***Fine***" (end).

Rhy. Fig. • Label used to recall a recurring accompaniment pattern (usually chordal).

Riff • Label used to recall composed, melodic lines (usually single notes) which recur.

Fill • Label used to identify a brief melodic figure which is to be inserted into the arrangement.

Rhy. Fill • A chordal version of a Fill.

tacet • Instrument is silent (drops out).

 • Repeat measures between signs.

 • When a repeated section has different endings, play the first ending only the first time and the second ending only the second time.

NOTE: Tablature numbers in parentheses mean:
1. The note is being sustained over a system (note in standard notation is tied), or
2. The note is sustained, but a new articulation (such as a hammer-on, pull-off, slide or vibrato begins), or
3. The note is a barely audible "ghost" note (note in standard notation is also in parentheses).